Original title:
A House of Secrets

Copyright © 2025 Creative Arts Management OÜ
All rights reserved.

Author: Dante Kingsley
ISBN HARDBACK: 978-1-80587-220-7
ISBN PAPERBACK: 978-1-80587-690-8

Fireside Secrets and Forgotten Dreams

In shadows flicker laughter's glow,
A hidden stash of tales to stow.
The cat's conspiracies, a furry scheme,
Chasing whispers like a wild dream.

Old shoes and hats make quite the mess,
Each one holds a quirky guess.
A dancing sock, a fridge full of cream,
Sprinkled with spice, a silly theme.

The creaky floorboards, they squeak and moan,
Revealing secrets in a jolly tone.
What mischief lies behind closed doors?
Giggling ghosts, and imaginary wars!

With every crackle from the fire's light,
Forgotten dreams take wing in flight.
A treasure map made of toast and jam,
Lies in wait, as silly as a pram.

Murmurs of the Past

In the attic, dust bunnies dance,
Whispers of chaos, given the chance.
A cat that tells tales of silver and gold,
While grandma sneezes at stories retold.

Paintings that giggle, they wink with delight,
In shadows they plot every starry night.
A vacuum cleaner's grumble does conspire,
To chase away secrets with stylish attire.

The Ghosts We Keep

Old socks in the dryer, they conspire to flee,
Holding a council and sipping on tea.
A ghost with a sense of humor quite rare,
Tells knock-knock jokes with a curlicue flair.

Framed photos that smirk when you're not around,
Cackling softly, they're quite the fun crowd.
With each creak of the floor, they giggle in glee,
"We're bored of this life, come join us for tea!"

Unseen Stories in Shattered Glass

Mirrors reflect what they want us to see,
An old shoe with a tale of adventure for free.
Shattered glass chuckles, it's sharp but it's true,
Each fragment reveals a wild rendezvous.

A lamp that's still buzzing with gossip of yore,
Hushed secrets collide as they spill on the floor.
In every old window, there's laughter in dreams,
Tales hidden in curtains, or so it all seems.

Tapestries of Deception

A rug that conceals a mishap or two,
Dancing around with a dust-covered shoe.
The fridge hums a tune of misplaced debate,
Over who made the casserole—oh, what a fate!

Curtains that flutter, they hold hands with lies,
They chat every evening, they revel, they rise.
Behind every panel, a riddle or rhyme,
In this comical house, we're out of our time.

The Silence Between the Beams

In the attic, dust bunnies play,
While the cat walks in, doing ballet.
Old trunks creak, tales untold,
Whispers of socks and treasures of old.

A ghostly laugh hangs in the air,
As the clock chimes loud without a care.
Unruly socks, mismatched and bright,
Laughing at secrets hidden from sight.

Threads of Forgotten Memories

A needle's eye winks at the past,
Stitched together, but these seams won't last.
Grandma's quilt, with patches so funny,
Hides secrets sweeter than honey.

Curtains flutter with a cheeky glance,
While old portraits pull off a dance.
Each thread sings a zany tune,
With memories that make us swoon.

Beneath the Veil of Wallpaper

Floral patterns hide next door,
Making faces, oh what a chore!
Aliens plot under faded prints,
While the dog tries to chase his hints.

The wallpaper peels at the edge,
Revealing tales on a secret ledge.
Each fold a laugh, a hidden jest,
Where the whispers of chaos rest.

The Key to Closed Doors

In the drawer, keys clink and rattle,
To rooms where wild socks have a battle.
It's a jungle gym made of shoes,
Where the sock's adventures amuse.

Unlocking doors with a mischievous grin,
Revealing chaos that fits right in.
Behind each closed door, a laugh we'll find,
In a place where peace and pandemonium bind.

Echoing Laughter from the Attic

In the attic where dust bunnies play,
Old chairs whisper tales of yesterday.
A box of socks, mismatched and bold,
Dance to the tunes of secrets untold.

A mirror reflects a crooked grin,
While cobwebs weave funny stories within.
The lanterns flicker with cheeky delight,
As shadows twirl in the pale moonlight.

Fables of the Hearth

By the fireplace, the embers glow,
Tales of the cat who fancied a show.
He leapt on the couch with a grand little spin,
But ended up tangled and wearing a grin.

The kettle sings tunes of mischief and cheer,
While dust motes dance in the light, oh dear!
With stories so silly, they make you chuckle,
Fables of warmth, in a cozy huddle.

Worn Pages of the Past

Books on the shelf with covers askew,
Whisper of secrets they once knew.
Pages yellowed, but laughter remains,
Each line a treasure of whimsical gains.

A fox in a cloak, quite dapper, no doubt,
Winks at the reader mid pout and shout.
Stories of curious cats, oh so sly,
In a world where dancing mice just might fly.

Lock and Key Memories

In a drawer, a key sits, forgotten and small,
It might open magic, or just a tall wall.
Behind every door, a giggle could swell,
What might be hiding? Only time will tell!

Lost socks and old toys play peek-a-boo,
Chasing the ghosts of a funnier view.
With giggles and grins tucked away in each nook,
Unlocking the laughter in every old book.

The Linger of Voices

In the attic, laughter hides,
Echoes of old jokes collide.
A parrot sings tales of woe,
While the cat plots down below.

Socks remember every fight,
Who stole the last bite of delight.
Ghostly giggles fill the air,
As dust bunnies plot somewhere.

Muffled Truths and Torn Pages

Books stacked high, their spines worn,
Whispers of love, sarcasm sworn.
Dog-eared secrets, laughter and tears,
Ink blots hiding all their fears.

Each page a riddle, each word a jest,
Stories tucked in a feathered nest.
A memoir of mischief, a laugh gone wild,
In stays the wisdom of a childish mind.

The Haunting of Memory

Old photos grin from dusty frames,
Winking at us, playing games.
The dog wore glasses, the cat had a tie,
Ghosts of the past all stopping by.

Each memory dances in silly delight,
Tickling our brains in the dead of night.
Who stole the cake? Was it Aunt Lou?
Or was it the mouse who wore a shoe?

Hushed Whispers of Once Was

Behind closed doors, secrets swirl,
A sock puppet shares with a twirl.
The garden gnome, with a cheeky grin,
Knows where all the mischief's been.

In corners and nooks, the tales abide,
With giggles and snorts, they will not hide.
A hidden stash of cookie crumbs,
Echoes of laughter always hums.

Cluttered Truths

In the kitchen lies a spoon,
That whispers tales of cheese and moon.
Old socks in piles tell tales so wild,
Of monsters dancing, all amused and riled.

Chairs stacked high with mystery's might,
Debate if cats can really take flight.
The closet hums a forgotten tune,
As dust bunnies cha-cha, under the moon.

Unspoken Words in the Walls

The walls are thick, with laughter and sighs,
They hold the secrets, with sly little eyes.
Hiccups and giggles around every turn,
With tales of old ghosts—less spooky, more fern.

Paint peels off, like a skin that forgot,
The dance of the years, what trouble was brought.
Underneath the floorboards, a ruckus awakes,
Sasquatch and frogs cooking pancakes.

The Hidden Diary

Found in a drawer, all tattered and torn,
It speaks of donuts, with sprinkles adorned.
Doodles of dragons, and ice cream galore,
Pirates who battle, then dance on the floor.

Funny little scribbles, rhymes that are whacky,
Poems about pets who are utterly tacky.
Each line a giggle, a heartfelt surprise,
Written in crayon, with big, silly eyes.

Forgotten Candles

In the corner, a candle sits,
Once bright with laughter, now it just skits.
It tells of parties, with wobbly chairs,
And pie fights that led to ecstatic stares.

Drippy and old, it longs to ignite,
To light up the chaos, bring back the night.
With scents of vanilla, it starts to spin tales,
Of birthday balloons and boisterous gales.

Whispers in the Wallpaper

In corners where the shadows dwell,
Old secrets giggle, can you tell?
The wallpaper peels, it starts to chat,
While mice debate, 'Who's fatter than that?'

The creaky floorboards jump and squeak,
Conspiring whispers, quite unique.
The light bulbs flicker, dance with glee,
Saying, 'Have you heard? It's a wild spree!'

Traces of the Unrevealed

Beneath the rug, a sock lies deep,
Mysteries abound, my secrets keep.
The cat stares hard, her tail's in a twist,
What's in the closet? A ghost or a mist?

The old hat hangs with a lopsided grin,
Telling stories of the fun it's been.
The fridge hums softly, whispers of pie,
Do leftovers laugh? Oh me, oh my!

Unlocked Secrets of the Past

The attic's full of treasures old,
Box of trinkets, stories untold.
A teddy bear wearing a frown so wide,
Did he miss a party? Did they really hide?

Beneath the floor, some gum is stuck,
Did a kid's mischief bring this bad luck?
The photos giggle with faces bizarre,
Who knew Granny danced with a rock star?

The Lattice of Lies

Behind the curtains, secrets weave,
Tangled stories that never leave.
The lamp light flickers, plays with the truth,
A conspiracy hatched by the squirrels of youth.

In the cupboard, a pot sings a tune,
While spoons gossip about the moon.
The walls bend close, they whisper and sigh,
Shhh! Don't tell the dog, or he'll start to cry!

Cobwebs of Time

In corners dark where shadows creep,
Are tales that make the bravest weep.
A dusty chair, a creaky floor,
Whispers of what was before.

Old photos grin with awkward poses,
Where mystery lies in blooming roses.
The dog barks loud at nothing near,
Is that a ghost or just a deer?

Underneath the squeaky stair,
A box of secrets hides somewhere.
Old letters tied with fraying string,
What chaos did those missives bring?

With every step, a giggle sounds,
As laughter echoes 'round the grounds.
These storied walls, with secrets rife,
Hide a humorous, zany life.

The Uninvited Guest

In shadows lurks a friendly ghost,
Who only shows up when we boast.
He giggles loud, then sneezes twice,
And says our jokes aren't very nice.

We leave the cookies out to share,
Yet find them gone, oh how unfair!
Instead he leaves his silly notes,
With doodles and outlandish quotes.

The cat rolls eyes, uncaring still,
As laughter echoes through the chill.
We set a place, it feels so right,
For our uninvited guest tonight.

So raise a toast to spirits near,
Who cheer us on throughout the year.
With every laugh and every jest,
This house keeps company—at best!

Layers of Paint and Pain

Behind the wall of old blue hue,
A secret's hiding, who ever knew?
Flakes of color peel away,
To reveal a story gone astray.

Each layer tells of things long past,
Of wild parties and games amassed.
Yet underneath the shining gloss,
Lives the memory of the loss.

We once found love in bold bright strokes,
Now we laugh at the silly blokes.
For every paintbrush wielded low,
The laughter helped our worries go.

So let's embrace the chipped and worn,
And tell the tales that still adorn.
With brushes dipped in joy and glee,
These whispered secrets set us free.

A Tapestry of Lies

Threads woven tight with laughter spun,
Whimsical secrets weigh a ton.
The fabric tells of mishaps grand,
Where truth gets tangled by the hand.

Each stitch a tale, each knot a prank,
In colors bright, it's truly rank!
An uncle danced, tore down a shade,
While waiting for grandma's lemonade.

A tapestry that sways and whirls,
With funny truths and backward twirls.
For every patch, a story told,
Of mischief, laughter, and hearts bold.

So gather 'round, let's take a peek,
At every lie, the fun we seek.
In threads of joy, we'll find our place,
As secrets dance in this warm space.

Unraveling the Threads

In the attic, spiders spin,
Old quilts whisper tales of sin.
Mismatched socks and broken toys,
Ghostly echoes of lost joys.

A cat named Whiskers, wise and sly,
Knows all the secrets creeping by.
He winks at ghosts, a playful tease,
As they trip over dust bunnies with ease.

A hidden stash of candy bars,
Lies tucked between the rusty jars.
Each bite a laugh, a fleeting thrill,
Like finding socks on the windowsill.

Underneath the creaky floor,
A giggle swells, then spills out more.
What lies beneath, we can't quite see,
But laughter's the key to mystery.

The Key That Never Turned

A rusty key upon the shelf,
It won't unlock the locked-up self.
With every twist, it mocks my dreams,
Like hiccups in the middle of screams.

I tried it on the bathroom door,
And swore I heard a ghostly roar.
Perhaps it guards a treasure rare,
Or just the scent of grandma's hair.

Each drawer I tug, a silent sigh,
For socks that seem to multiply.
Unlocking laughter, what a chore,
As socks escape to roam the floor.

A search for secrets, fun but wild,
Like hide-and-seek with a wayward child.
In every nook, the giggles stir,
Where humor hides, and secrets blur.

Lanterns in the Darkness

Through the halls, the lanterns sway,
Lighting up the ghosts at play.
Each flicker sparks a grin so wide,
As shadows dance, they don't dare hide.

In the closet, a treasure trove,
Of mismatched shoes and tales to wove.
A sock puppet troupe starts to sing,
As chaos takes flight on gentle wing.

The attic's filled with laughter's song,
Ghostly whispers won't last long.
With every glow of candlelight,
The silly secrets spring to life.

So let the laughter echo loud,
Among the spirits, brave and proud.
In corners dark, where giggles bloom,
A funny tale loves to loom.

Dusty Corners of Memory

In dusty corners, stories thrive,
Of mischief where the laughter dives.
A rogue chair spins with tales untold,
Of silly pranks from days of old.

The vacuum's roar, a dreadful beast,
That swallows crumbs of snack-time feast.
But forgotten fries and candy wraps,
Join in the dance and form some maps.

Old photo albums gleam with glee,
Flashing smiles that just can't be.
Each face a riddle, a joyful lore,
Of family secrets, less is more.

Through every giggle, we can find,
The joy that's in the stories lined.
In dusty nooks, we clear the air,
And find our laughter hiding there.

The Envelopes of Silence

There's a drawer stacked high with notes,
All marked with scribbles and silly quotes.
What do they mean? Oh, who can tell?
I laugh at secrets kept so well.

A toast to the truths that no one knows,
Like Auntie's cat who wears her clothes.
In this room, the laughter always peaks,
As we shuffle through those paper freaks.

It's a jolly tomb of long-lost schemes,
Plans for parties and ice cream dreams.
Every envelope a winking face,
Invites to long-forgotten space.

So grab a chair and lend an ear,
As we share our gags and hearty cheer.
For every secret has its jest,
In this wacky world, we're truly blessed.

The Bygone Heartbeat

In the corner there's an old guitar,
Covered in dust, it traveled far.
Once it strummed a lover's tune,
Now just echoes in the afternoon.

With each strum, a ghost may dance,
A love affair that lost its chance.
Yet in its strings, a chuckle lies,
As it wonders where that songbird flies.

And I found a shoe, one left alone,
Its partner long gone, a tale unknown.
Was it left behind in a playful race?
Or did it seek a better space?

Laughter lingers in the captive air,
As memories swirl like a wild fair.
Maybe one day, it'll all come back,
With a song, a shoe, and a hearty snack!

Hidden among the Pages

In the attic, a book with a nutty tale,
Tells of pirates, but it's filled with kale.
Every page, from cover to cover,
Leaves us giggling, we can't recover.

Between the lines, a cat takes naps,
Sipping tea from tiny laps.
As plots twist and silly tales unfold,
I'm convinced this book is pure gold.

There's a map sketched in crayon bright,
Leading to treasures of pure delight.
But we discovered it only leads,
To last week's pizza and yesterday's seeds!

So gather 'round for a tale so sweet,
Of mismatched socks and fantastic feet.
For in these pages, pure fun resides,
With every flip, laughter abides.

Whispers in the Walls

Behind the wallpaper, secrets dwell,
Trading gossip like a spinning cell.
These whispering walls are quite the crowd,
They giggle and snicker, oh so loud!

Each creak and groan is a punchline,
As we dance to the sound in fine design.
Who knew that a house could be so bright,
With the spirit of joy taking flight?

A painting of a dog, with a haughty glare,
Barks out jokes that hang in the air.
Is it a dog or some fancy spy?
Oh, the mystery makes the giggles fly!

So here's to the house of chortles and fun,
Where laughter outshines the warming sun.
With each secret and chuckle, we see,
This wacky home's a comedy spree!

Doorways to Yesterday

In the attic, dust goes wild,
Old toys laugh like a carefree child.
Pictures whisper from the walls,
Behind the door, a ghostly brawl.

Sock puppets dance on the floor,
Chasing memories out the door.
Laughter echoes with every creak,
What secrets do the floorboards sneak?

A hidden diary, dog-eared and worn,
Details of pranks from long ago born.
We played tag with the moonlight's glow,
Where did those days of wonder go?

In corners dark, mischief hums,
Jars of candy, of laughter, of crumbs.
Doorways twist and lead us back,
To find the joy that we seem to lack.

The Echo of Unsaid Goodbyes

Behind the curtain, secrets hide,
A rubber chicken, a curious guide.
Grandpa's socks and grandma's tea,
Echoes giggle, can you hear me?

In the drawer, a note I find,
Of silly pranks, and one-of-a-kind.
Cups that clink, old spoons that jive,
In this home, old jokes come alive.

The cat's got stories, a tail to tell,
Of misplaced hats and an old love spell.
Echoes whisper as we reminisce,
Unsaid goodbyes wrapped in laughter's kiss.

Cheese curls scattered on the floor,
Where did we leave our jokes galore?
Every corner holds a tale,
With giggles stacked like mail.

A Chamber of Echoes

In the pantry, laughter blooms,
Cookies giggle in their loamy tombs.
Under the sink, the sponges plot,
Mischief brews in the secret hot pot.

A hat with feathers, a shoe on the shelf,
Turns out, the boots dance all by themselves.
Whispers rustle like autumn leaves,
What nonsense inside this chamber achieves?

Cobwebs flutter, like they're in a play,
The lamp encourages a wobbly ballet.
Step into the echo and hear the cheer,
Of the secrets that linger year after year.

Through the hallways, giggles roam,
Echoing tales of a brief wander home.
In every room, a chuckle hides,
In every cabinet, a joke abides.

The Forgotten Letters

Beneath the stairs, who could have guessed,
A box of letters, funly compressed.
Postcards from places nobody knows,
Requesting chicken from phantom crows.

The ink has faded but the laughter gleams,
Love notes exchanged in ridiculous schemes.
"Dear friend, I've captured a pie in the sky,"
Endless giggles at the sky-high lie.

Each page unfolds a new goofy twist,
Dinner invitations upon a tryst.
Scribes of silliness, tales of delight,
In forgotten letters, joy takes flight.

So gather the stories, joyous and loud,
Read them aloud to a giggling crowd.
In these words, we forever dwell,
As echoes of laughter cast their spell.

Dusty Albums and Locked Drawers

In the attic, dust bunnies play,
Old albums hide tales of yesterday.
Photos of people with silly grins,
Each snapshot whispers of hidden sins.

Locked drawers creak with a secret laugh,
Mismatched socks tell a curious path.
A diary once held dreams of a queen,
Now it's full of doodles, quite obscene.

Grandma's old hat with a feathered plume,
Winks at the socks that dance in the gloom.
With each turn of a page or a key,
We giggle at tales from history.

The mysterious jar filled with buttons galore,
Each one a treasure, each one a score.
In this nook of hides and playful pride,
Laughter calms the secrets inside.

The Riddle of Sheltered Souls

Who lives behind the curtain's swish?
A cat or a witch, or perhaps a fish?
The closet door creaks, what might it hide?
A mischief-maker, filled with pride.

Every shelf's a riddle wrapped tight,
Old toys that squeak in the middle of night.
On a rainy Sunday, they come alive,
Chasing the echoes of secrets they thrive.

In the corner, an old shoe sits still,
Filled with crumpled notes of a forgotten thrill.
Each scribble tells stories of days gone by,
With laughter and whispers that flutter and fly.

Wandering through rooms of playful lore,
Finding the giggles behind every door.
In this puzzle of laughter, lies the goal,
The joy of the secrets, of sheltered souls.

Faint Footsteps in the Night

Faint footsteps echo, a playful chase,
The cat tippy-toes, embracing the space.
Beware of the creaks, the laughter's near,
What mischief awaits? Grab a snack, my dear!

In shadows and whispers, they'll soon appear,
Socks on the floor, aren't they a cheer?
The midnight brigade of giggles in flight,
Stirring the tales of the sleepy night.

A tickling breeze makes the curtains sway,
As tiny hands dance, then swiftly away.
What's lost in the cupboard, what's hiding below?
A treasure trove, or a sneaky toe?

The clock's laughing tune, the moon's gentle light,
Shadows twist with the hint of delight.
In the stillness, the stories ignite,
Faint footsteps 'round, finding pure insight.

The Map of Concealed Lives

A crinkly map, hidden in plain sight,
Marks secret spots where laughter ignites.
Under the staircase, a treasure's in wait,
Twinkling with secrets that giggle and skate.

Each dot a tale, a hidden sweet stash,
Chocolate crumbs and an unexpected flash.
Dive beneath couches, delve into drawers,
The laughter erupts as the chaos explores.

In the backyard, a fort made of dreams,
With sticky fingers and wild, free schemes.
Each leaf a whisper, each rock a friend,
Secrets bubbling, never to end.

So off with the map, let's find our way,
Through giggles and grins, come what may.
In a world cloaked in laughter, lives intertwine,
Concealed, yet revealed, by design divine.

Beneath the Floorboards

Under the planks, mice giggle and play,
While old shoes chuckle in a snoring display.
Dust bunnies trade tales of what they have seen,
As the woodworms compose in a joyous routine.

Each night they gather for a wild, grand feast,
Leftover crumbs from the chaos at least.
The sofa is a throne, so plush and so proud,
Where the dust mites perform, quite lively and loud.

The cat stands guard, but he's fast asleep,
Dreaming of fish that would make his heart leap.
The secrets of laughter are hidden just there,
Behind the old door, in the soft, creaky air.

Attuned to the Unseen

In the attic, a sock puppet holds court,
With a crown made of lint and a very short skirt.
They plot wicked pranks with the dolls on the shelf,
All while the old broom just laughs at itself.

The ghosts do the cha-cha; they take up the space,
Swapping their stories with comical grace.
While the vacuum's a monster, all hungry and bold,
For crumbs of the dinner, left over and cold.

In the corners, the shadows are having a ball,
Telling tall tales of the time they saw Paul.
He danced with the spider who spun a fine web,
While the ceiling fan whistled a tune to the ebb.

The Keeper of Silent Stories

The bookshelf has secrets it'll never confess,
Holding whispers of love wrapped in papered stress.
A tome in the corner, it snickers at fate,
As the lamp tries to flicker, it knows it's too late.

With bookmarks around as best friends in disguise,
Though they mock the old tome with its fading goodbyes.

A cat naps atop, with a mischievous grin,
While the pages conspire to bring tales back in.

The kettle starts to whistle, a ruckus it makes,
Startling the book into jumps and mistakes.
The stories come alive with a hint of delight,
While the teapot giggles, "That's a tale for tonight!"

Windows to the Hidden Past

The panes look out with a wobbly grin,
At messes they've seen and the chaos within.
They frame the young cousins, who giggle and run,
While shadows dance subtly, just having their fun.

With each creak and crack, they whisper a plot,
Sharing old dramas by the little green pot.
The curtains are gossipers, swaying with flair,
Hiding old treasures, if anyone dares.

Through the glass, the ghosts peep with a smile,
Doing the moonwalk and staying awhile.
The world outside is simple, but laughter can soar,
As memories tug at the frame of the door.

Footprints Left in the Dust

In the corner, a cat plots,
With a mouse that's not really a mouse.
The dog's in on it, but forgot,
As he snoozes under the couch.

Footprints lead to the pantry,
Where cookie crumbs dance like stars.
A trail of giggles, oh so zany,
What's next? A circus of jars?

Dust bunnies twirl in delight,
As we tiptoe to the great unknown.
Each creak of the floor brings a fright,
Who knew a broom could be a throne?

Laughing echoes can be found,
In shadows, mischief night and day.
With every silly little sound,
Secrets hide in a playful way.

Fragments of Forgotten Laughter

In the attic lies a lost joke,
Tangled in spider web and gloom.
Each giggle a forgotten poke,
Like a rogue clown in a costume.

The old chair squeaks with a grin,
As echoes of laughter rebound.
A cat leaps high, it's a win,
While the clock just spins round and round.

Fractured tales on dusty shelves,
Items whisper, 'we too have fun!'
A sock puppet lost in itself,
Dances 'til the day is done.

In the corners, mischief brews,
Like soup left boiling on the stove.
What secrets new can we amuse?
In laughter's realm, we freely rove.

The Labyrinth of Silent Sighs

Whispers float like feathers light,
Through hallways lined with painted glares.
Tick-tock, the clocks seem to fight,
As secrets glide through hidden stairs.

Mismatched shoes hide in the dark,
While the walls breathe in playful fear.
Each turn reveals a funny spark,
Will the ticklish ghost appear?

Chairs hold court with their own tales,
As shadows plot with velvet paws.
Laughter rides on dusty trails,
Making mischief without flaws.

Silent sighs made of pure jest,
Bouncing 'round like softest dreams.
In this maze, we're truly blessed,
With humor hidden in the seams.

The Portraits that Watch

Eyes follow as you sneak a bite,
From the snack jar hiding away.
Each portrait grins in dim twilight,
Can they join in the jokes we play?

A lady in lace once spilled tea,
Now giggles haunt her painted lips.
She knows all our secrets, you see,
Lurking near the candy-tape strips.

The gentleman points at a new hat,
As if to say, 'You look quite sour.'
But in truth, he's just a cool cat,
Counting laughs with utmost power.

With every glance, they conspire,
Painting our antics on the wall.
In this gallery of the quire,
We laugh, we play, we thieve it all.

Ciphers Amongst the Furnishings

In the corner, a chair that squeaks,
Might just spill all the secrets it keeps.
A lamp that flickers when no one's near,
Could it be hiding a ghostly cheer?

Dust bunnies roll like whispers of old,
Underneath cushions, tales are told.
Cushions dance when the cats play fair,
Are they laughing at what's hidden there?

A clock that ticks in an odd little way,
Counts down the moments till secrets play.
Figures lurk in shadows of night,
Who knew the couch could cause such a fright?

So if you sit on the sofa with glee,
Listen close, who knows what you'll see?
Perhaps a waltz from an unseen band,
As the furniture moves to its own little hand.

Flickers of a Lurking Past

In a nook where no one dare to glance,
Photos flicker like a ghostly dance.
Mirrors quirk with a smirk or two,
Reflecting tales of a different view.

A painting's eyes seem to follow you,
As if they know all that you've been through.
Every step echoes with a soft giggle,
Could it be just a dust-covered wiggle?

The hallway creaks like it has a tale,
Of socks that vanished and bread left stale.
A laugh in the pantry, a scream from the loo,
Just the house playing its charming view.

So traipse about with a curious heart,
Each wall whispers secrets, a laugh or a start.
Be careful where you tread in the night,
You might just join in on the ghostly light!

Unseen Footsteps on the Stairs

Footsteps stomp and then softly fade,
Little ones giggle, a ghostly parade.
Socks go missing, lost to the sneaks,
Who would have thought a sock thief tweaks?

The stairs are a stage for a playful show,
Echoes abound of long-lost woe.
With a creak and a clatter, they join the play,
As spirits sidestep in their own array.

Sneaky shadows flit here and there,
Life of the party, do you dare?
As you climb, remember the funs,
For every step could lead to runs!

So next time you rise, give them a cheer,
For laughter and whispers are always near.
These stairs hold a jolly tryst,
In this quirky house, you can't resist!

The Gaze of the Unrevealed

Watchful eyes seem to linger here,
Painted folks grinning from ear to ear.
They gather 'round for tea and laughs,
What tricks do they hide in their crafts?

A curtain twitches in the breeze,
Did someone peek to see you sneeze?
Noses and throats feel rather dry,
Are they just waiting for you to cry?

Chairs converse in hushed tones so sweet,
Children chatter from under the seat.
Each corner feels like a comic scene,
Where every hidden nook's a routine.

So pull up a chair and stay awhile,
In this castle of quirks, find your smile.
For with every glance and every jest,
You might just find you're a honored guest!

Whispers Behind Closed Doors

In the hall, a creaky floor,
Secrets tumble, laugh and snore.
'What's that noise?' the cat asks me,
Whiskers twitching, curious as can be.

Behind the door, a giggling spree,
Grandpa's jokes, a mystery key.
The goldfish winks, a sly little wink,
While shadows dance and candles blink.

Squeaky hinges, tales untold,
With every crack, we laugh so bold.
But when you peek, all is still,
Just shoes and dust, an empty thrill.

Yet we strain to hear the giggle,
A riddle wrapped in every wiggle.
What tales the walls could surely share,
If only we dared to stop and stare.

Shadows in the Attic

Up in the attic, who knows what's there?
A pirate's hat, a teddy bear.
Old trunks sit with lids askew,
Did Aunt Edna hide a voodoo brew?

Ghosts of cats play hide and seek,
Scratches, thumps, an eerie squeak.
I swear I saw a sock go by,
Or was that just a clever lie?

The shadows giggle, a friendly tease,
Mismatched boots, and a puzzle, please!
Each corner holds a joke or two,
Echoes of laughter, old and new.

Among the dust, we're right at home,
Fables find us, we laugh and roam.
In a world of wonders, nothing seems wrong,
Just a sleepy attic where we belong.

The Portraits Speak

On the wall, with painted grace,
Grandma's portrait, a knowing face.
She whispers tales through crooked smiles,
Of stolen pies and playful wiles.

Uncle Joe in a pirate's guise,
Winks at me with mischief in his eyes.
Another one in a fancy hat,
Asks about my first pet cat.

Each frame a story, laughter brewed,
Max, the dog, always seems to brood.
Between the brushstrokes, a flicker of fun,
In every sigh, they've already won.

A family gathering stuck in time,
Their chuckles rise with every chime.
Oh, how they chat without a sound,
In this gallery, joy is found.

Echoes of the Forgotten

Echoes rippling in the air,
Whispers of trouble, joy, and care.
Forgotten toys, they spring to life,
Playing pranks amid the strife.

Squeaky voices, tales unfold,
Of secret clubs and treasures bold.
A rubber chicken, a wayward hat,
Guess who lost it? The old pet cat!

Beneath the stairs, mischief runs wild,
Remember the time we all played child?
Tripped on shoes while giggling loud,
We painted the walls and made our crowd.

Now the echoes bring back the spark,
Of all the joy in a memory's arc.
Through time and laughter, we're never alone,
In every echo, our spirits have grown.

Breathe Life into the Locked Room

Inside the closet, a cat does nap,
Mysterious shadows warp the map.
A ticklish ghost tickles your toes,
His giggles echo as the doorknob froze.

With pizza slices behind the door,
And dance parties on the kitchen floor.
Each room's a riddle we love to crack,
Where even dust bunnies plot their attack.

Suspicious stains on the kitchen rug,
Could it be sauce, or a rogue bug?
Sometimes it feels like who lives where?
The walls may whisper but we just glare.

In the attic, a hat winks back,
One-eyed jokes in our own little track.
As laughter tumbles like marbles in a game,
For fun is the treasure, we stake our claim.

The Weight of Hidden Echoes

Behind closed doors, laughter sneaks,
With each whispered tale, the fun peaks.
A broomstick plays the clowning trick,
And chairs do dance when things get slick.

Old portraits stare, with shifty eyes,
Whispering secrets, oh what a surprise!
What's that in the attic? A closet of socks?
Or a treasure map drawn by a fox?

Is that a ghost with a rubber chicken?
Or just Uncle Joe with a joke that's kickin'?
Every crack in the wall hums a tune,
And the cupboards tap-dance under the moon.

With echoes that quack like ducks on a spree,
This place is wild, and it's all for free!
So let's open the drawers and look for fun,
In this zany house, the laughter's just begun.

Secrets Carved in Wood

In the woodwork, stories swirl and spin,
Each knot and grain, where do we begin?
A chair that creaks might just have a tale,
Of dancing raccoons with cupcakes to hail.

The table's surface shows remnants of fights,
With crumbs of laughter from late nights.
A secret compartment, snug and neat,
Hides a collection of odd socks and feet.

Here's a cupboard full of tiny toys,
Where imagination bursts with joyous noise.
And on the shelves, all the dust bunnies play,
Making sure we see them at the end of the day.

So let's carve some laughter into the grain,
For these wooden secrets will never wane!
Each knot is a giggle waiting to burst,
In this wacky home, we'll always be first.

The Garden of Whispers

In the garden, whispers twirl like vines,
Where the veggies gather and converse in lines.
"Is that a carrot or a sneaky spy?"
And the tomatoes nod, giving it a try.

The daisies gossip about the buzzing bees,
And the sunflowers laugh in the summer breeze.
With mushrooms that giggle, hidden from sight,
As pansies plan a prank under the moonlight.

"Oh, what a weed!" cries the hose with glee,
"I'll water the secrets, come dance with me!"
This garden grows stories that swirl and twine,
Each petal a secret, delicious and fine.

So let's dig up laughter among the greens,
For here in the garden, anything's seen.
With whispers and giggles, we nurture the love,
In this leafy haven, we soar like a dove.

The Cryptic Graffiti of Life

In the attic, dust bunnies spin,
Whispers of laughter trapped within.
A sock on the ceiling, a shoe on the wall,
It's all a grand puzzle, or just a free fall.

Unexpected art in the living room space,
A cereal box mural, what a wild place!
With crayons and chaos, the walls come alive,
Where every strange mark is a secret to thrive.

The fridge holds a tale of old lunch plans,
Mayo and mustard doing a dance.
Each shelf is a treasure, it bursts with delight,
Not a single dull moment hides from plain sight.

So grab a snack, take a look around,
In this comedy house, odd treasures abound.
With giggles and quirks, we unlock every door,
In this whimsical realm, who could ask for more?

The Unlocked Diary of Days Long Past

Dusty pages filled with silly rhymes,
A tale of mishaps across silly times.
Spilled grape juice on a cat's fluffy tail,
And Grandma's lost wig that rolled down the trail.

Each crumpled note is a giggle burst,
Of pranks gone wrong, or fates that reversed.
A high-flying kite that got stuck in the tree,
Or socks gone rogue; they just wanted to be free.

Forgotten treasures in corners around,
Old toys and trinkets waiting to be found.
These memories spark giant smiles on our face,
As we dance through the past, at our own crazy pace.

We turn every leaf, laughter filling the air,
With secrets so silly, we can't help but share.
Each scribble tells tales that make our hearts glow,
In this diary of time, the joy always flows.

An Enigmatic Embrace

Beneath the old quilt, secrets hide tight,
With whispers of dreams far out of sight.
The cat curls up with a knowing glance,
What mischief awaits in this whimsical dance?

Couches are portals to lands of delight,
Where cushions become monsters in a pillow fight.
In the hug of a blanket, we giggle and squirm,
With laughter as fuel, the giggles confirm.

The door creaks open with a scratchy tune,
As we plot our next caper under the moon.
A world of fun in every shadow and nook,
Where every embrace tells the wildest of books.

So join the commotion, the silly parade,
In this cozy abode, where memories are made.
With each hug we share, the room fills with cheer,
In this quirky retreat, it's magic we steer.

Voices in the Haze of Memory

Echoes of laughter don't fade away,
In corners they chatter, come out to play.
A spoon in the drawer sings songs of old,
While forks share tales that were never retold.

The clock on the wall tics with a grin,
As if it holds secrets of all that's been.
Baking disasters where flour took flight,
Are recalled as legends that still spark delight.

Grandpa's old stories hand down like gold,
Of mischievous elves that were cheeky and bold.
With giggles of ghosts that dance in the air,
These whimsical whispers are joyfully rare.

So lean in real close, let the memories flow,
In the haze of the past, the magic will grow.
With every sweet voice, we cherish and cheer,
In this funny old space, all the love's crystal clear.

Shadows Beneath the Floorboards

Beneath the creaky wood so bold,
Little mice gather tales untold.
They dance and they prance without a care,
While humans search for long-lost hair.

They chuckle at socks left out to dry,
And giggle at snacks that humans deny.
In gaps and cracks, their secrets thrive,
As they plot ways to keep dreams alive.

Mice wear small hats made of cheese,
While humans sneeze from dust with ease.
They peek out from nooks with a grin,
Squeaking of parties they've thrown within.

So hear the whispers beneath your feet,
Of furry friends and their tasty treats.
In the shadows, laughter finds its way,
Where secrets of mice come out to play.

Echoes of Unspoken Truths

In corners where the shadows dwell,
The echoes giggle, casting a spell.
They tell of odd socks, a curious case,
And missing cookies that vanish without trace.

The closet holds a laughter spree,
With shirts that poke and poke with glee.
Every creak from the floor does tease,
As it whispers jokes carried on the breeze.

Beware the drawer that won't stay shut,
It swallows secrets with a giggle and strut.
Shoes that dance when no one's around,
In the silliness where joy is found.

So when you hear a chuckle soft,
Know there's mischief stirred aloft.
In each unspoken truth, a wink,
The joyful moments—don't you think?

Hidden Corners, Hidden Lives

In the tiny nooks where whispers play,
Tiny creatures plot their day.
Dust bunnies roll like furry balloons,
Recounting tales of old cartoons.

Underneath the stairs where shadows loom,
A gathering held in the forgotten room.
All the forgotten toys have fun,
Making memories until they're done.

The clock ticks slow, but don't you fear,
For time plays tricks with laughter near.
As secrets swirl in breezy drafts,
Hidden corners hold their heartfelt laughs.

Surprises wait in every bend,
With playful spirits that never end.
So peek in the dark, let curiosity thrive,
In the hidden lives where joy arrives.

Secrets in the Attic

Up in the attic, oh what a sight,
Old hats and toys hold tales of delight.
A chest filled with dust, laughter brews,
As the old wooden floor starts tapping its shoes.

A suitcase that claims it's been around,
Hiding treasures and whispers profound.
With every open, a giggle escapes,
As they share the most ridiculous tapes.

The ghost of last year's Halloween,
Waves with a grin, a ghastly scene.
He juggles old masks made of cheese,
And tells of mishaps that bring to tease.

So when you climb those creaky stairs,
Listen closely, you might hear their flares.
In secrets found, fun lights the way,
In the attic tales where mischief plays.

Photographs of Ghostly Moments

In dusty albums, pictures lie,
Of Aunt Maude's cat who learned to fly.
A ghostly grin on every face,
But where's the punchline in this place?

A spectral selfie, oh what fun,
With Uncle Bob and his pet gun.
They wink and pose with quirky flair,
Just who is standing over there?

A blurry figure, quite the joker,
Is it a ghost or just a smoker?
We laugh and share our ghostly tales,
As hiccups drown in eerie wails.

In haunted laughter, secrets roam,
Each snapshot taken feels like home.
We cherish quirks, embrace the glee,
In photographs of mystery.

What Lies Behind the Staircase

There's often whispers in the hall,
About the mystery behind the wall.
Could it be treasure? Could it be snacks?
Or just the sound of old men's hacks?

Torn between myth and a cat's purr,
Each creak has me quaking—what's the stir?
Yet laughter bubbles, it's just the cat,
Conspiring with ghosts for a midnight chat.

I peek and see a sandwich left,
Now that's a secret quite deft.
What if stairs held more than dust?
A snack buffet—oh, that's a must!

So here we wait, the curious bunch,
For midnight meals, and ghostly lunch.
What lies behind, we can't quite guess,
Yet all agree it's quite a mess!

The Scent of Forgotten Vows

In the attic, the smell of cake,
Leftovers from a wedding break.
The vows were whispered, 'til they burst,
With laughter so sweet, the echoes cursed.

A soggy bouquet, wilted yet spry,
Hitches a ride as we ask why.
Did bride and groom escape their fate?
An adventure gone, oh, isn't it great?

Old letters smudged with icing's stain,
Confessions lurk in gooey gain.
'Run away!' shouted cakes in fright,
As we danced under the pale moonlight.

The scent of vows, long overdue,
Brings giggles and slicing, a frosted view.
In forgotten moments, sweet and grand,
We feast on laughter, hand in hand.

The Hushed Echo of Laughter

A hallway echoes with childish glee,
Where laughter thrived and came to be.
Yet shadows weave in depths of play,
What mischief lurked at end of day?

Behind closed doors, a prank awaits,
An echo stirs, it laughs and hates.
In beds of secrets, truths collide,
With every giggle they try to hide.

Don't mind the rumbles, it's just the chair,
Wobbling with whispers, unaware.
Who dares to peek in a ghostly spree?
Just a pair of socks and a cup of tea.

And so we sit, our secrets thick,
A hush of laughter, a playful trick.
In walls that murmur, joy resides,
Through echoes that refuse to hide.

An Archive of Shadows

In the corners where dust bunnies play,
Lurking whispers giggle all day.
What's that under the old chair?
A sock, or perhaps a lost pair?

Behind the shelves, a great book shakes,
Joking about all its silly mistakes.
I heard it snicker, the old tome,
Wishing it could just go home.

The attic hides treasures and fears,
A jumbled mess of old souvenirs.
A doll with a smirk, and a cat with a grin,
What tales would they tell if they could begin?

Light flickers and shadows dance around,
Each creak and crack is a hiding sound.
Secrets abound in this playful place,
Where laughter and mystery always embrace.

Beneath the Shingles

Beneath the shingles, a secret lies,
A family of squirrels wearing ties.
They hold meetings on rainy days,
Planning their nutty escapades and plays.

The roof chatters in giggles and squawks,
As chimney smoke does the funky talks.
Who knew the raindrops could take a dive?
Jumping from leaves like they're still alive?

Some say a ghost roams the hallway wide,
But it's just a cat taking a pride stride.
With a flick of her tail, she claims her throne,
The ruler of secrets, and all alone.

Under the eaves where whispers thrive,
A band of mice keeps the tales alive.
They squeak of treasures and crumbs from the past,
In this roofed-up fun fest, they forever last.

Secrets in the Garden

In the garden, a gnome with a grin,
Hides secrets with a mischievous spin.
He tells of flowers that dance at night,
Underneath the moon's soft, silver light.

The carrots gossip with the old scarecrow,
Sharing tales of the plants that grow.
"Watch out for the weasel!" the tomatoes shout,
As they plot to keep their secrets out.

A hedgehog in glasses scribbles low,
Documenting all the gossip, you know.
The daisies twirl in their fragrant breeze,
Charming the bees with their sweet tease.

With each rustle, a story unfolds,
Of mischief and mysteries that never grow old.
In the soil, where the playful hearts dwell,
The secrets bloom, oh so very well.

The Rustle of Hidden Pages

In a library where shadows play tricks,
Books find their voice and share their kicks.
A volume quips from the very last shelf,
"I've read more stories than you read yourself!"

The ancient tomes plan a bookish prank,
While poetry hums in a soft, sweet tank.
The romance novels plot their next twist,
Hoping to be the one that can't be missed.

Dusty corners hold conversations sweet,
As the characters come alive on their feet.
A novel sighs, "Let's rewrite the end,"
As the tales intermingle and play pretend.

With each rustle and flipping of the leaves,
A riot of laughter the paper achieves.
Secrets spill like ink on a page,
In this whimsical world of literary stage.

Beneath the Steps

Underneath the stairs, what do we find?
A sock or a shoe, left behind in a bind.
A ghostly old cat with an eye for mischief,
Guarding treasures lost, its grin far too swift.

Creaky wood groans as we tiptoe near,
Whispers of secrets waft through the air.
An ancient cheese whizzes past like lightning,
Poking fun at the often fright-fighting.

Beneath the Gaze of the Portrait

A portrait hangs crooked, with eyes like a hawk,
    Watching us giggle, it starts to talk.
"I've seen all your pranks, not one has escaped,
You'll rue the day you thought you could tape!"

With a wink, it glimmers, oh how we all laugh,
    Sharing our ruckus, a silly old gaffe.
    The secrets it holds beneath layers of paint,
Might just be a rhyme, or a life's little complaint.

The Sighs of the Midnight Wind

At midnight the wind lets out a loud sigh,
It tickles the curtains, wings ready to fly.
Through windows it whistles, a prankster so sly,
Stealing our snacks while we all just comply.

It wraps 'round the corners, with laughter like bells,
Asking for secrets, spilling all that it tells.
A game of hide and seek in the chill of the dark,
Whispering mischief, but always with a spark.

Flickering Shadows of the Unrevealed

Shadows dance wildly on walls with a glee,
Playing tag with our fears, come join if you see.
They whisper in tones that snicker and tease,
Daring us to laugh, not just on our knees.

Under the moonlight, they slide to and fro,
Beneath each soft flicker, there's plenty to show.
Chasing our giggles, they'll twirl and they'll leap,
Keeping us guessing, a laughter to reap.

Cracks in the Foundation

There's a creak in the floor, a squeak in the door,
My cat hides in shadows, she's plotting for more.
The wallpaper whispers, it's out for a lark,
It tells all the tales when the sun starts to dark.

Beneath the floorboards, a stash of old shoes,
Mismatched and forgotten, they're bearing the blues.
They dance in the night with a laugh and a spin,
They'd claim they were stylish, if only they'd win.

The attic's a stage for the dust bunnies' play,
In costumes of cobwebs, they dress up each day.
If you peek through the rafters, it's quite the surprise,
Their antics are funny, but who sees their eyes?

Behind every curtain, a tale to be told,
Of socks with no partners, and mirrors so bold.
The secrets are silly, yet make me feel fine,
In this crazy old house, the joy's by design.

Beneath the Surface of Paint

The walls wear a story, so thick and so bright,
Each layer a secret, like cake in the night.
I swore I saw movement, a brushstroke's delight,
Then splattered some frosting, oh what a fright!

Underneath all the layers, there's laughter, I hear,
A chorus of colors, like they're sipping beer.
With each stroke I make, they start to protest,
'A peach on the porch? That's simply the best!'

The ceilings keep gossip, from square to round,
They'll chuckle and whisper, 'til the paint hits the ground.

"Just choose a fun color, let's make it a spree,"
They beg with a giggle, "Let's brighten our spree!"

So let's splash the tones in this playful retreat,
Where secrets are silly, and color's the beat.
In a world made of laughter, with paint I'll unite,
These walls hold a wonder, so gay and so bright.

The Light That Never Shone

There's a bulb in the corner, it's covered in dust,
It swears it once sparkled, it's aching to bust.
But when flicked on low, it merely just hums,
Like crickets at night, it's just full of dumb trums.

In a room full of shadows, it flickers and sighs,
It tells all the secrets of lost alibis.
A clown in the corner, with paint peeling off,
It chuckles each night, 'Just lighten up, scoff!'

The lamp on the desk has a bulb that's so bold,
It lights up like sunshine, with stories untold.
But when it gets quiet, it winks with a glee,
"Oh please, don't be serious, just laugh with me!"

So here in this space, where the light dims so low,
There's fun in the corners, with shadows that glow.
Let's dance with the phantoms, we'll make them our friends,
In a glow of the goofies, let not humor end.

Quiet Confessions at Dusk

The chairs start to whisper, in soft evening tones,
With secrets of laughter, and playful old groans.
They confide in the shadows as dusk begins creeping,
"We're tired of silence, let's start up some peeping!"

The walls have their stories, they bubble with glee,
About times when the cake proved less sweet than the tea.

The floorboards are giggling, they can hardly contain,
An elephant's dance that so broke their refrain!

The windows, they chuckle, at moonlight's embrace,
A staged soirée where all shadows find grace.
They sway round the room, an exquisite ballet,
In whispers of daylight that gently gave way.

So join in the fun, as the night comes alive,
With secrets and chuckles, let silliness thrive.
In the heart of the dusk, where confessions are sweet,
Let laughter be heard, it's a wonderful treat!

The Secret Beneath the Chimney

There's a ruckus in the flue,
Where raccoons brew their nightly stew.
They wear hats made of old tin foil,
And throw dance parties on the soil.

The dust bunnies hold their court,
In the halls where secrets cavort.
They gossip of treasures long lost,
And laugh at the chaos they've tossed.

A sock puppet plays the clown,
As the broomsticks waltz around town.
With a jiggle and jig, they all collide,
In this attic where laughter can't hide.

Next time you sit by the hearth,
Listen close to the warmth and mirth.
You may just find with a peek or two,
A raucous world waiting for you!

Veils of Opacity

In corners where shadows creep,
Lies a mystery, oh so deep.
A dog sniffs out socks from the void,
While cats plot schemes to be enjoyed.

Behind curtains, the whispers flare,
Of secrets born from daily care.
With each creak of the old floorboard,
Even the mice seem to record.

The kitchen's filled with phantom cooks,
Who bake mishaps from dusty books.
A pie that jiggles, a cake that pouts,
All come with silly little doubts.

So if you step into this den,
Prepare for laughter, time and again.
For in every corner of this space,
Are hijinks that time can't erase!

The Map of Hidden Rooms

With a quill made of chicken bone,
I scribbled maps when I was alone.
In the pantry, 'neath jars of jam,
Lurks the legend of Uncle Sam.

The laundry's a maze, a true delight,
Where shirts go missing, out of sight.
And every lost sock has a tale,
Of wild adventures beyond the pale.

One room is neon, filled with glee,
The sound of tickles, a sight to see.
Kids play hide and seek with ghouls,
While the vacuum cleaner breaks all the rules.

So gather your friends, let's explore,
This house that holds secrets galore.
With each step comes another surprise,
In rooms where laughter never dies!

Conversations with Silence

In the quiet, there's a jest,
That whispers to the heart's behest.
A chair that squeaks, a wall that sighs,
Chasing echoes 'neath the skies.

The clock ticks in a rhythmic dance,
Trying hard to take a chance.
While shadows play a game of peek,
Trading stories they dare not speak.

The fridge hums tales of yesterday,
Where leftovers hold a grand buffet.
Salads argue with the leftover stew,
And spaghetti dreams of things it can do.

So embrace the hush, let it spin,
Find joy in the chaos within.
For when silence talks, it's quite the treat,
A giggle found at the hidden seat!

Secrets in the Cellar

In the cellar where spiders crawl,
Old jars of pickles line the wall.
A grinning rat with a top hat on,
Sips his tea 'til the break of dawn.

Dusty crates filled with things unknown,
Whispers of rubber chickens moan.
A sock collection of wild design,
Each pair missing, oh what a crime!

A ghost of cake calls me to play,
With icing smiles that never decay.
We dance with shadows, laugh in delight,
In this crazy place, all feels so right.

So if you hear giggles beneath your feet,
Join the fun, it's a silly treat.
In this cellar where secrets do dwell,
It's a party, do come, you'll do well!

The Clock That Ticks Too Loud

There's a clock that ticks with such great flair,
It giggles and whispers, it doesn't care.
Each tick-a-tock brings chatter 'round,
As it dances atop the nightstand's crown.

At midnight, it tells the world it's late,
With a bouncy jig, it just can't wait.
"If you can catch me!" it joyfully teases,
As its hands spin like wild tornado breezes.

The neighbors complain, their sleep is naught,
They reckon it's madness, they're quite in thought.
But the clock just chuckles, "What's your big deal?
Life's too short not to tick with zeal!"

So here's to the clock that loves to be loud,
With its quirks and twirls, it's really quite proud.
A symphony played on the walls of the night,
Making our dreams dance in pure delight!

Shadows in the Hallway

In the hallway where shadows play,
They make silly faces throughout the day.
One's a penguin, another a cat,
Having a party—imagine that!

They sneak and they peek 'round the corners with glee,
Waving their arms as they laugh with me.
A friendly ghost with a feathered bow,
Swoops in for hugs, "Come join the show!"

Picture frames sway as they dance in time,
To a song so catchy, it's truly sublime.
With each tiny tap, and a flip of the wrist,
These mischievous shadows bloom in the mist.

So if you wander down this sweet hall,
Join the antics of shadows, give them a call.
With giggles and wiggles, they'd love your kin,
In the world of silliness, let the fun begin!

The Ghosts of Yesterday

The ghosts of yesterday, dressed in flair,
Whirl like confetti in the autumn air.
With polka-dot trousers and top hats so wide,
They twirl through the rooms, distinctly untried.

Each one tells tales of mischief and play,
From knocking on windows to hiding away.
With jellybean snacks that they share with delight,
They'll phantom you up for a ghostly good night.

Did you hear the one about the shoe with no mate?
It danced 'round the room till it met up with fate.
Now it wobbles and giggles with each silly step,
Creating a ruckus, that little inept!

So don't be afraid of these playful spooks,
With laughter and joy, they're your newest flukes.
Join their antics, lose track of the years,
With the ghosts of yesterday, there are no fears!

www.ingramcontent.com/pod-product-compliance
Lightning Source LLC
Chambersburg PA
CBHW060113230426
43661CB00003B/171